Quilting the
Great Outdoors

LANDAUER BOOKS

Quilting the
Great Outdoors

by Debbie Field
for Granola Girl™ Designs©

Copyright© 2003 by Landauer Corporation

Projects Copyright© 2003 by Debbie Field

This book was designed, produced, and published by Landauer Books
A division of Landauer Corporation
12251 Maffitt Road, Cumming, Iowa 50061

President/Publisher: Jeramy Lanigan Landauer
Vice President Sales & Marketing: James L. Knapp
Editor-in-Chief: Becky Johnston
Creative Director: Laurel Albright
Project Editor: Patty Barrett
Photographer: Craig Anderson and Dennis Kennedy
Photostylists: DeWayne Studer and Laurel Albright

ISBN: 1-890621-60-9
This book is printed on acid-free paper.
Printed in China

10 9 8 7 6 5 4 3 2 1

INTRODUCTION

If you're in love with quilts that depict the great outdoor nostalgia, this book is for you.

Celebrate Lewis and Clark's 200th anniversary of their spectacular journey by creating your own treasured keepsake quilt featuring many of the sights and scenery of the noted explorers' trek.

Featured on the following pages you'll find quilts and projects with easy-to-follow instructions and patterns for quilting the great outdoors—an exciting adventure focused on woodland wildlife, mighty oaks and acorns, and nature's splendor—all inspired by my love of the great outdoors.

Choose a favorite appliquéd wildlife scene for a small project or capture the essence of several blocks to create one spectacular wildlife habitat quilt. I hope that you will enjoy quilting the great outdoors as much as I do!

Debbie Field

About
the Artist

Debbie Field produces her work through Granola Girl Designs®. She is world-renowned for her textile designs, authored books, and published patterns.

Her enthusiasm toward nature and outdoor family activities are the inspiration for her fabric designs and quilts. She looks at the outdoors as her reference library—an open book to endless resources of color, texture, and wildlife. Taking photos or sketching a scene is the start of a new quilt or fabric line. At the end of her outdoor workday, she reflects on how she enjoys the best of both worlds. Working outside and the excitement of creating new quilts and fabrics.

Debbie's quilts and fabric lines appeared in national magazines and other publications. Her quilts have also won awards. She attributes her success to her father who instilled an adventurous outdoor lifestyle for his family.

Contents

Nature's **Splendor** 90

General Instructions

Assemble the tools and supplies to complete the project. In addition to basic cutting and sewing tools, the following will make cutting and sewing easier: small sharp scissors to cut appliqué shapes, rotary cutter and mat, extra rotary blades, and a transparent ruler with markings.

Replace the sewing machine needle each time you start a project to maintain even stitches and to prevent skipped stitches and broken needles during the project. Clean the machine after every project to remove lint and to keep it running smoothly.

The projects shown are made with unwashed fabrics. If you prewash fabrics, purchase extra yardage to allow for shrinkage. The 100-percent cottons and flannels used in the wilderness quilts and accessories are from Debbie's Granola Girl™ collections: Marble Cake Basics, Wilderness Kids, and Out of the Woods fabric lines manufactured by Troy Corporation. Ask for them by name at your local quilt shop.

Please read through the project instructions before cutting and sewing. Square the fabric before cutting and square it again after cutting 3 or 4 strips. Align the ruler accurately to diagonally cut squares into triangles. Sew with 1/4" seam allowances throughout, unless stated otherwise in the instructions, and check seam allowance accuracy to prevent compounding even slight errors. Press seams toward the darker fabric when possible. When pressing small joined pieces, press in the direction that creates less bulk.

Basic Appliqué

Please note that the printed appliqué templates are reversed. Trace and cut the templates as printed, unless the illustrations and photos indicate to reverse the templates. For appliqués that face the opposite direction, trace and reverse the template. Dashed lines indicate design overlap.

Trace the appliqué template to the fusible webbing with a fine tip marker or sharp pencil, allowing space to cut 1/4" beyond the traced lines. Position the fusible web on the wrong side of the appliqué fabric. Follow the webbing manufacturer's instructions to fuse the webbing to the fabric. Allow the fabric to cool and cut along the traced line. Remove the paper backing and follow the pattern placement to position the appliqué pieces on the background fabrics.

Use lightweight tear-away stabilizer to machine appliqué. Place the stabilizer beneath the fabric layers and use a small, zigzag stitch to sew around each shape, smoothly covering the raw fabric edge. If your machine has stitch options, use them to detail appliqués. After the stitching is complete, remove the stabilizer according to the manufacturer's instructions.

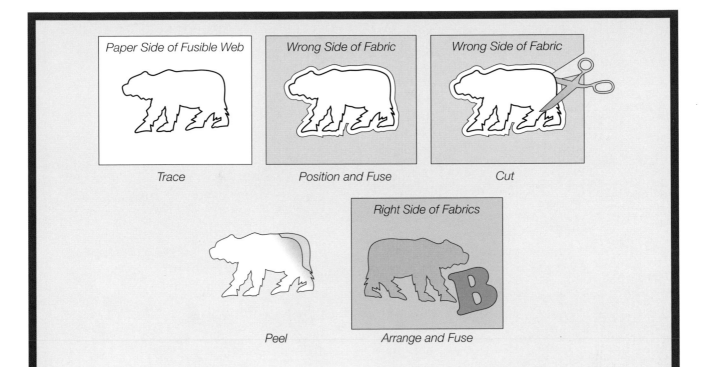

Trace — Paper Side of Fusible Web

Position and Fuse — Wrong Side of Fabric

Cut — Wrong Side of Fabric

Peel

Arrange and Fuse — Right Side of Fabrics

Basic **Binding**

Join binding strips for a continuous length. Fold the strip in half lengthwise, right sides out, and press. Match the raw edges of the folded strip to the quilt top, along a lower edge and approximately 6" form a corner, allowing approximately 6" free to join to the opposite end of the binding. Avoid placing binding seams on corners. Sew the binding to the quilt top with a 1/4" seam allowance (see Step 1).

At the first corner, stop 1/4" from the corner, backstitch, raise the presser foot and needle, and rotate the quilt 90 degrees. Fold the binding back onto itself to create a miter (see Step 2), then fold it along the adjacent seam (see Step 3), matching raw edges. Continue sewing to the next corner and repeat the mitered corner process. Where the binding ends meet, fold under one binding edge 1/4", encase the opposite binding edge, and stitch it to the quilt top.

Trim the batting and backing fabric even with the quilt top and binding. Fold the binding strip to the back of the quilt and handsew it in place with a blind stitch. Sign and date the quilt, including the recipient's name if it is a gift.

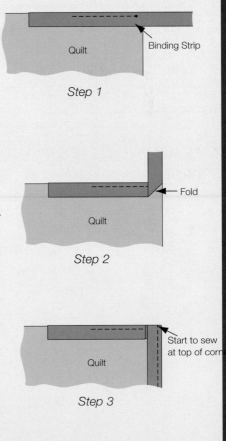

Step 1 — Quilt, Binding Strip

Step 2 — Quilt, Fold

Step 3 — Quilt, Start to sew at top of corner.

Woodland Wildlife
Curved Top Quilt

(Finished size 58" x 88" approximately)

MATERIALS

1-7/8 yards	Tan Print for Background Fabric
1-1/4 yards	Black Tone-on-Tone for Sashing and 1st Border Fabric
1-7/8 yards	Dark Gold Print for 2nd Border Fabric
7/8 yard	Dark Gold Print for Binding
6 yards	Backing
64" x 94" piece	Batting

APPLIQUÉ FABRICS

Large Acorn Fabrics

1/2 yard	Light Green Marble for Large Acorn Bottoms
1/4 yard	Tan Print for Large Acorn Tops
6" x 9" piece	Brown Marble for Large Acorn Stem Bottoms
2" x 4" piece	Dark Brown for Large Acorn Stem Tops

Small Acorn Fabrics

5" x 5" piece	Medium Brown for Small Acorn Bottoms
5" x 5" piece	Dark Brown for Small Acorn Tops

Bear Block Fabrics

4" x 6" piece	Black Marble for Bear
3" x 7" piece	Gold Marble for Ground and Bear Nose
10" x 16" piece	Medium Green Marble for Blueberry Leaves
5" x 5" piece	Blue for Blueberries
4" x 10" piece	Dark Brown Marble for Oak Leaves on Acorn

Buffalo Block Fabrics

4" x 4" piece	Brown Marble for Buffalo Body
4" x 4" piece	Black Marble for Buffalo Body Front and Head
3" x 9" piece	Plum Marble for Mountains
1" x 1" piece	Cream for Buffalo Horn
9" x 12" piece	Gold Marble for Aspen Leaves
5" x 5" piece	Green Marble for Aspen Stems
4" x 8" piece	Green Marble for Oak Leaves on Acorn

Elk Block Fabrics

5" x 5" piece	Medium Brown for Elk Body
3" x 4" piece	Dark Brown for Elk Head
3" x 3" piece	Cream for Front Elk Antlers

3" x 3" piece	Brown Marble for Back Elk Antlers
2" x 2" piece	Cream for Elk Tail
2" x 7" piece	Green Marble for Ground
4" x 8" piece	Green Marble for Oak Leaves on Acorn
10" x 20" piece	Gold Marble for Pin Oak Leaves

Fish Block Fabrics

5" x 5" piece	Green Marble for Fish Body
2" x 2" piece	Light Green Marble for Fish Mouth
3" x 3" piece	Coral for Fish Belly
1" x 1" piece	White for Fish Eye
6" x 7" piece	Dark Blue Marble for Large Water
3" x 5" piece	Medium Blue Marble for Small Water
12" x 14" piece	Green Marble for Pine Sprigs
4" x 10" piece	Light Brown Marble for Pine Cones
4" x 8" piece	Rust Marble for Oak Leaves on Acorn

Moose Block Fabrics

5" x 6" piece	Dark Brown Marble for Moose Body
3" x 4" piece	Medium Brown Marble for Moose Head
3" x 5" piece	Cream Print for Front Rack
3" x 4" piece	Light Brown Marble for Back Rack

4" x 10" piece	Medium Green for Oak Leaves on Acorn
8" x 16" piece	Dark Green Marble for Large Oak Leaves
2" x 6" piece	Blue Marble for Ground

Wolves Block Fabrics

10" x 12" piece	Black Marble for Wolves
3" x 7" piece	Green Marble for Ground
8" x 16" piece	Dark Rust Print for Maple Leaves
3" x 3" piece	Gold for Moon

Curved Top Border Fabrics

5" x 7" piece	Light Tan Print for Elk Antlers
5" x 6" piece	Dark Brown for Elk Head
10" x 35" piece	Medium/Light Green Marble for Medium Trees
6" x 12" piece	Medium/Light Green Marble for Small Trees
8" x 11" piece	Dark Green Marble for Large Tree
7 yards	HeatnBond®—Lite

Sulky® threads to match appliqués

Stabilizer – Lightweight (Tear-away)

NOTE: *Fabrics are based on 42"-wide fabric that has not been washed. Please purchase accordingly.*

Cutting Instructions

From Tan Print:
- Cut 3 strips—20" x 42";
  from strips cut
  6—20" x 20" squares.

From Black Tone-on-Tone:
- Cut 10 strips—3-1/2" x 42".

From Dark Gold Print:
- Cut 6 strips—5-1/2" x 42".
- Cut 2 strips—9-1/2" x 42".
- Cut 1 strip—5" x 42".

From Gold Print for Binding:
- Cut 8 strips—3" x 42".

Assembly

1. Refer to the appliqué placement and the general instructions in the front of the book to fuse and position the appliqué pieces to the tan print quilt blocks. Use a small zigzag stitch and matching thread around each shape to appliqué it to the quilt block. Remember to use tear-away stabilizer for stitching appliqués.

2. After the quilt blocks are appliquéd, resquare the blocks and trim so all 6 blocks are the same size.

3. Measure the quilt blocks through the center and cut 3 strips that length from 2 of the 3-1/2" x 42" Black Tone-on-Tone sashing strips.

4. Sew the sashing strips to the appliquéd blocks, as shown below. Press toward the dark. You will have 3 rows of 2 blocks and a sashing strip.

5. Measure the rows through the center for sashing length. Use 4 strips from the 3-1/2" x 42" sashing strips and cut to the length needed. Sew the rows together, as shown. Press toward the dark.

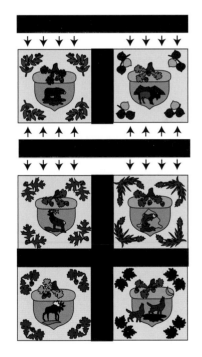

6. Measure the quilt top lengthwise through the center for the measurement of the side border strips. Cut 2 strips to the length needed using the remaining 3-1/2" x 42" black tone-on-tone sashing strips. Sew to each side as shown, *next page upper left*. Press toward the dark.

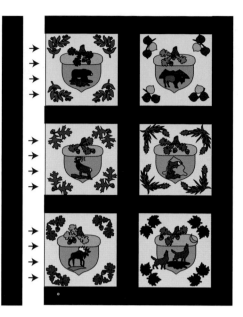

7. Measure the quilt top widthwise through the center for the measurement of the bottom border strip. Diagonally piece two Dark Gold Print 5-1/2" strips and cut the length needed. Sew the strip to the bottom as shown, *below*. Press toward the dark.

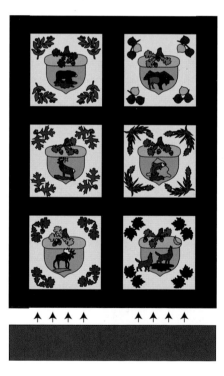

8. Measure the quilt top lengthwise through the center for the measurement of the side border strips. Diagonally piece 2—5-1/2" Dark Gold Print strips for each side and cut the length needed. Sew to each side as shown *upper right* and press toward the dark.

9. Find the center of the 5" x 42" Dark Gold Print and trace the curved template on strip and stitch on the drawn line. Set aside until Step 11.

10. Measure quilt top through the center widthwise for top border length. Cut the Dark Gold Print 9-1/2" 2nd border strip that length.

11. Find the center of the top 9-1/2" border strip. Place the center of the curved border strip to the center of the 9-1/2" border strip. Sew the 2 pieces together and press toward the 9-1/2" strip CAREFULLY.

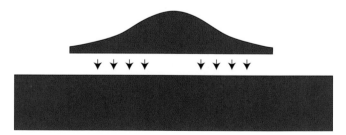

12. Refer to the appliqué placement and the general instructions in the front of the book to fuse and position the appliqué pieces to the quilt border. Use a small zigzag stitch and matching thread around each shape to appliqué it to the quilt border. *Take great care while appliquéing so your border does not get stretched.*

13. Sew the border on quilt top and press toward the dark. Now cut along the drawn and stitched line of top of quilt.

14. Layer the quilt backing fabric, batting, and quilt top. Baste the layers together. Hand-or machine-quilt as desired. Finish the quilt by sewing on the binding following the steps in the general instructions at the front of the book.

Curved Top Quilt

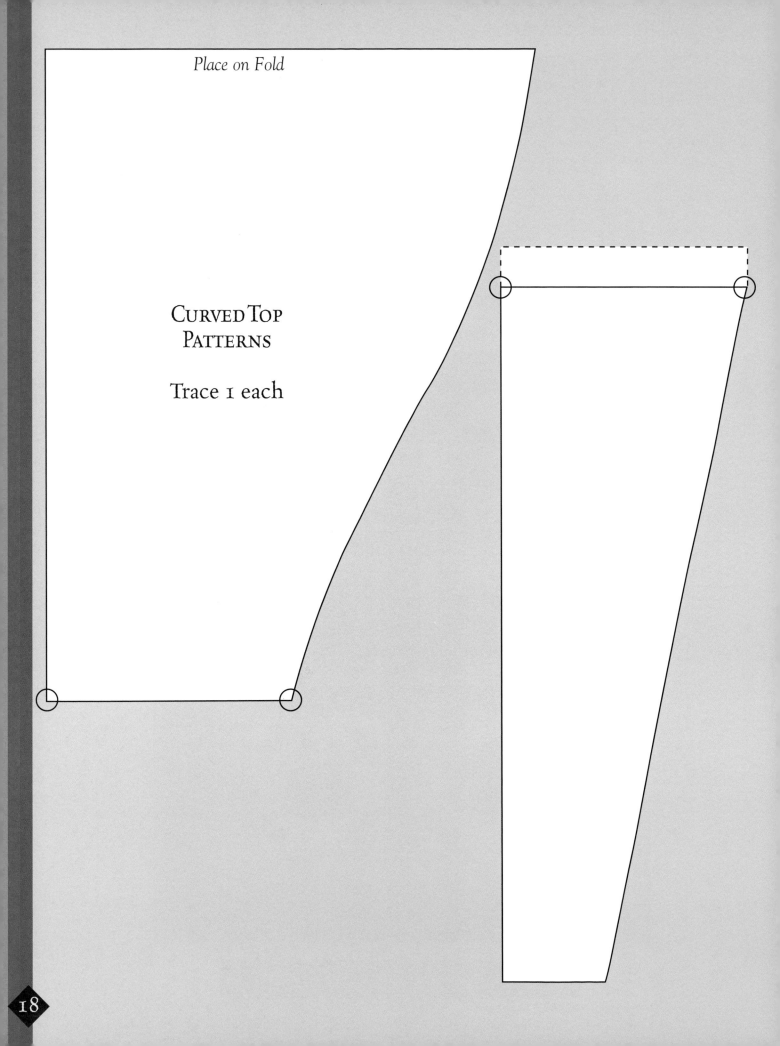

Place on Fold

CURVED TOP PATTERNS

Trace 1 each

Place on Fold

LARGE ACORN
-*Stem Top & Bottom* (Trace 6)
-*Large Acorn Top & Bottom* (Trace 6)
-*Oak Leaf* (Trace 18)
-*Small Acorn Top & Bottom* (Trace 12)

Reverse 2

Bear Block
-Blueberries (Trace 24)
-Blueberry Leaves (Trace 4)
-Bear Body (Trace 1)
-Bear Nose (Trace 1)
-Ground (Trace 1)

Buffalo Block
-Aspen Stem (Trace 4)
-Aspen Leaves (Trace 12)
-Buffalo Body, Head & Horn (Trace 1)
-Mountain (Trace 1)

ELK BLOCK
-Acorn Top & Bottom (Trace 4)
-Elk Body, Head, Tail & Antlers (Trace 1)
-Pin Oak Leaf (Trace 8)
-Ground (Trace 1)

Reverse 2

FISH BLOCK
-*Pine Sprig* (Trace 4)
-*Pine Cones* (Trace 8)
-*Large Water* (Trace 1)

FISH BLOCK

-Fish Body, Eye, Belly and Mouth (Trace 1)
-Small Water (Trace 2)

Moose Block
- Moose Body, Head & Racks (Trace 1)
- Oak Leaf (Trace 8)
- Acorn Top & Bottom (Trace 4 each)
- Ground (Trace 1)

WOLF BLOCK
-*Maple Leaf* (Trace 8)
-*Moon* (Trace 1)
-*Wolf* (Trace 2)
-*Ground* (Trace 1)

ELK HEAD ON CURVED TOP
-Antlers (Trace 1 each)
-Elk Head (Trace 1)

Trees on Curved Top
-*Small Tree* (Trace 3)
-*Medium Tree* (Trace 5)

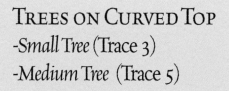

LARGE TREE PATTERN
(Trace 1)

(Finished size 61" x 83" approximately)

MATERIALS

1-7/8 yards	Light Green Print for Background Fabric
1-1/4 yards	Black Tone-on-Tone for Sashing and 1st Border Fabric
2-1/8 yards	Buffalo Check for 2nd Border Fabric
7/8 yard	Black Tone-on-Tone for Binding
5-1/4 yards	Backing
67" x 91" piece	Batting

APPLIQUÉ FABRICS

Large Acorn Fabrics

1/2 yard	Green Marble for Large Acorn Bottoms
1/4 yard	Tan Print for Large Acorn Tops
6" x 9" piece	Brown Marble for Large Acorn Stem Bottoms
2" x 4" piece	Dark Brown for Large Acorn Stem Tops

Small Acorn Fabrics

5" x 5" piece	Medium Brown for Small Acorn Bottoms
5" x 5" piece	Dark Green for Small Acorn Tops

Bear Block Fabrics

4" x 6" piece	Black Marble for Bear
3" x 7" piece	Gold Marble for Ground and Bear Nose
10" x 16" piece	Medium Green Marble for Blueberry Leaves
5" x 5" piece	Blue for Blueberries
4" x 10" piece	Dark Brown Marble for Oak Leaves on Acorn

Buffalo Block Fabrics

4" x 4" piece	Brown Marble for Buffalo Body
4" x 4" piece	Black Marble for Buffalo Body Front and Head
3" x 9" piece	Plum Marble for Mountains
1" x 1" piece	Cream for Buffalo Horn
9" x 12" piece	Gold Marble for Aspen Leaves
5" x 5" piece	Green Marble for Aspen Stems
4" x 8" piece	Green Marble for Oak Leaves on Acorn

Elk Block Fabrics

5" x 5" piece	Medium Brown for Elk Body
3" x 4" piece	Dark Brown for Elk Head
3" x 3" piece	Cream for Elk Front Antlers

3" x 3" piece	Brown Marble for Elk Back Antlers
2" x 2" piece	Cream for Elk Tail
2" x 7" piece	Green Marble for Ground
4" x 8" piece	Green Marble for Oak Leaves on Acorn
10" x 20" piece	Gold Marble for Pin Oak Leaves

Fish Block Fabrics

5" x 5" piece	Green Marble for Fish Body
2" x 2" piece	Light Green Marble for Fish Mouth
3" x 3" piece	Coral for Fish Belly
1" x 1" piece	White for Fish Eye
6" x 7" piece	Dark Blue Marble for Large Water
3" x 5" piece	Medium Blue Marble for Small Water
12" x 14" piece	Green Marble for Pine Sprigs
4" x 10" piece	Light Brown Marble for Pine Cones
4" x 8" piece	Rust Marble for Oak Leaves on Acorn

Moose Block Fabrics

5" x 6" piece	Dark Brown Marble for Moose Body
3" x 4" piece	Medium Brown Marble for Moose Head
3" x 5" piece	Cream Print for Moose Front Rack
3" x 4" piece	Light Brown Marble for Moose Back Rack

3" x 4" piece	Cream Print for Antlers
4" x 10" piece	Medium Green for Oak Leaves on Acorn
8" x 16" piece	Dark Green Marble for Large Oak Leaves
2" x 6" piece	Blue Marble for Ground

Wolves Block Fabrics

10" x 12" piece	Black Marble for Wolves
3" x 7" piece	Green Marble for Ground
8" x 16" piece	Dark Rust Print for Maple Leaves
3" x 3" piece	Gold for Moon
7 yards	HeatnBond®—Lite

Sulky® threads to match appliqués

Stabilizer – Lightweight (Tear-away)

NOTE: *Fabrics are based on 42"-wide fabric that has not been washed. Please purchase accordingly.*

CUTTING INSTRUCTIONS

From Light Green Print:
  • Cut 3 strips – 20" x 42"; from strips cut 6—20" x 20" squares.

From Black Tone-on-Tone:
  • Cut 10 strips – 3-1/2" x 42".

From Buffalo Check:
  • Cut 9 strips – 6-7/8" x 42".

From Black Tone-on-Tone for Binding:
  • Cut 8 strips – 3" x 42".

ASSEMBLY

1. Refer to the appliqué placement and the general instructions in the front of the book to fuse and position the appliqué pieces to the Light Green Print quilt blocks. Use a small zigzag stitch and matching thread around each shape to appliqué it to the quilt block. Remember to use tear-away stabilizer for stitching appliqués.

2. After the quilt blocks are appliquéd, resquare the blocks and trim so all 6 blocks are the same size.

3. Measure the quilt blocks through the center and cut 3 strips that length from 2 of the 3-1/2" x 42" Black Tone-on-Tone sashing strips.

4. Sew the sashing strips to the appliquéd blocks, as shown *below*. Press toward the dark. You will have 3 rows of 2 blocks and a sashing strip.

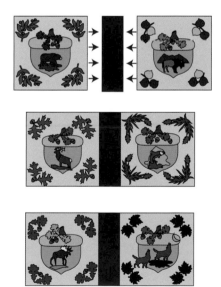

6. Measure the quilt top lengthwise through the center for the measurement of the side border strips. Cut 2 strips to the length needed using the remaining 3-1/2" x 42" Black Tone-on-Tone sashing strips. Sew to each side as shown *below*. Press toward the dark.

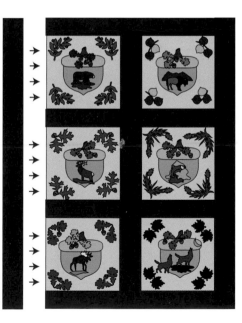

5. Measure the rows through the center for sashing length. Use 4 strips from the 3-1/2" x 42" Black Tone-on-Tone sashing strips and cut to the length needed. Sew the rows together, as shown *above right*. Press toward the dark.

33

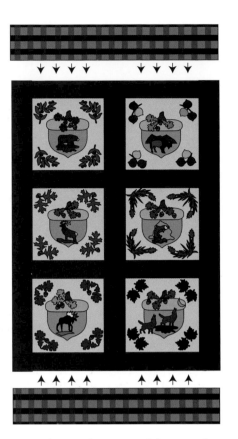

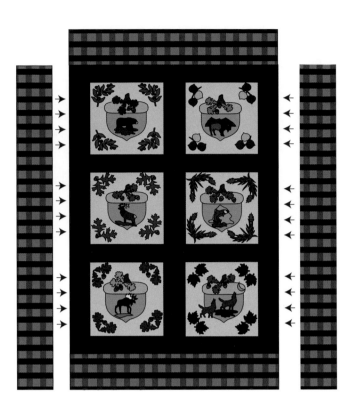

7. Measure the quilt top widthwise through the center for the measurement of the bottom border strip. Piece 2—Buffalo Check 6-7/8" strips and cut the length needed. Sew the strip to the bottom and top as shown *above*. Press toward the dark.

8. Measure the quilt top lengthwise through the center for the measurement of the side border strips. Piece 2—6-7/8" strips for each side and cut the length needed. Sew to each side as shown *above* and press toward the dark.

9. Layer the quilt backing fabric, batting, and quilt top. Baste the layers together. Hand-or machine-quilt as desired. Finish the quilt by sewing on the binding following the steps in the general instructions at the front of the book.

Buffalo Check Border Quilt

Place on Fold

LARGE ACORN
-*Stem Top & Bottom* (Trace 6)
-*Large Acorn Top & Bottom* (Trace 6)
-*Oak Leaf* (Trace 18)
-*Small Acorn Top & Bottom* (Trace 12)

(Reverse 2)

BEAR BLOCK
- *Blueberries* (Trace 24)
- *Blueberry Leaves* (Trace 4)
- *Bear Body* (Trace 1)
- *Bear Nose* (Trace 1)
- *Ground* (Trace 1)

Buffalo Block
- Aspen Stem (Trace 4)
- Aspen Leaves (Trace 12)
- Buffalo Body, Head & Horn (Trace 1)
- Mountain (Trace 1)

ELK BLOCK
-Acorn Top & Bottom (Trace 4)
-Elk Body, Head, Tail & Antlers (Trace 1)
-Pin Oak Leaf (Trace 8)
-Ground (Trace 1)

(Reverse 2)

Fish Block
-Pine Sprig (Trace 4)
-Pine Cones (Trace 8)
-Large Water (Trace 1)

Fish Block

-Fish Body, Eye, Belly and Mouth (Trace 1)

-Small Water (Trace 2)

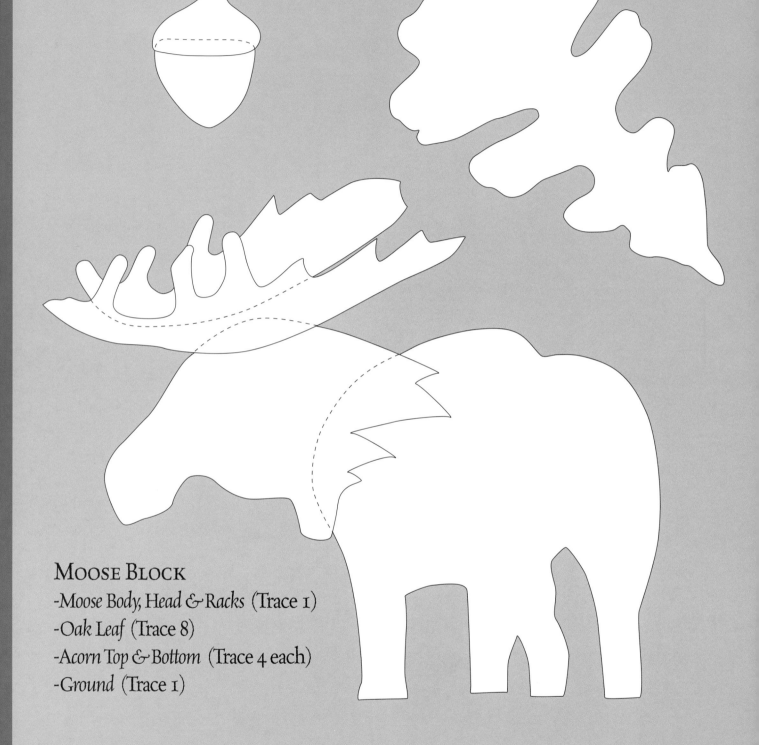

MOOSE BLOCK
-*Moose Body, Head & Racks* (Trace 1)
-*Oak Leaf* (Trace 8)
-*Acorn Top & Bottom* (Trace 4 each)
-*Ground* (Trace 1)

WOLF BLOCK
-*Maple Leaf* (Trace 8)
-*Moon* (Trace 1)
-*Wolf* (Trace 2)
-*Ground* (Trace 1)

Woodland Wildlife
Wallhanging

(Finished size 26" x 26" approximately)

MATERIALS

2/3 yard	Tan Marble for Background Fabric
1/2 yard	Dark Brown Marble for Border Fabric
3/8 yard	Dark Brown Marble for Binding
1 yard	Backing
31" x 31"	Batting

APPLIQUÉ FABRICS

3" x 3" piece	Dark Brown Marble for Elk Head
5" x 6" piece	Medium Brown Marble for Elk Body
4" x 4" piece	Light Tan for Front Antler & Tail Pieces
18" x 22" piece	Rust for Back Antler & Pin Oak Leaves
11" x 11" piece	Dark Green for Small Oak Leaves & Grass
4" x 12" piece	Gold Marble for Large Acorn Top
10" x 12" piece	Avocado Green Marble for Large Acorn Bottom
1 yard scraps	Small Acorn Tops, Bottoms, & Acorn Stem

1 yard	HeatnBond®—Lite

Sulky® threads to match appliqués

Stabilizer – Lightweight (Tear-away)

NOTE: *Fabrics are based on 42"-wide fabric that has not been washed. Please purchase accordingly.*

CUTTING INSTRUCTIONS

From Tan Marble:
- Cut 1 square – 20" x 20".

From Dark Brown Marble :
- Cut 3 strips – 3-1/2" x 42"; from the strips cut 2—3-1/2" x 20" rectangles and 2—3-1/2" x 26" rectangles.

From Dark Brown Marble for Binding:
- Cut 3 strips – 2-1/2" x 42".

ASSEMBLY

1. Sew the 3-1/2" x 20" strips to the sides of the background piece, as shown. Press toward the dark.

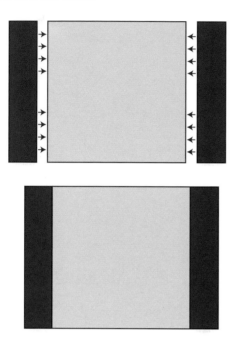

2. Sew the 3-1/2" x 26" strips to the top and bottom, as shown. Press toward the dark.

3. Refer to the appliqué placement and the general instructions in the front of the book to fuse and position the appliqué pieces to the quilt top. Use a small zigzag stitch and matching thread around each shape to appliqué it to the quilt top.

4. Layer the quilt backing fabric, batting, and quilt top. Baste the layers together. Hand- or machine-quilt as desired. Finish the quilt by sewing on the binding, following the steps in the general instructions at the front of the book.

ELK WALLHANGING
-Elk Body, Head, Tail & Antlers (Trace 1)
-Pin Oak Leaf (Trace 8)
-Grass (Trace 1)

LARGE ACORN

-*Stem Top & Bottom* (Trace 1 each)

-*Large Acorn Top & Bottom* (Trace 1 each)

-*Oak Leaf* (Trace 3)

-*Small Acorn Top & Bottom* (Trace 2 each)

Place on Fold

Elk Wallhanging

Woodland Wildlife
Table Topper

(Finished size 27" circle approximately)

MATERIALS

5/8 yard	Light Tan Print for Background Fabric
5/8 yard	Black Marble for Tongues Fabric
5/8 yard	Backing

APPLIQUÉ FABRICS

18" x 22"	Dark Green for Oak Leaves
18" x 22"	Light Green for Oak Leaves
8" x 8"	Brown for Head
6" x 6"	Medium Gold for Antler Front
5" x 5"	Dark Gold for Antler Back
6" x 6"	Dark Brown for Top
10" x 10"	Gold Acorn Bottom
7/8 yard	HeatnBond®—Lite

Sulky® threads to match appliqués

Stabilizer – Lightweight (Tear-away)

NOTE: *Fabrics are based on 42"-wide fabric that has not been washed. Please purchase accordingly.*

CUTTING INSTRUCTIONS

From Tan Print –
- Cut 1 square – 20" x 20".

From Black Marble –
- Cut 42 pieces (21 pairs) from Tongue pattern template.

From Backing –
- Cut 1 square – 20" x 20".

ASSEMBLY

1. With right sides together, fold the background square in half, as shown.

2. Fold the folded piece in half again, as shown.

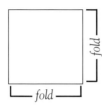

3. Place a straight pin with a medium–sized head in the corner where the 2 folds are, as shown in Diagram 1. Tie a knot with a piece of string that has been placed under the head of the straight pin. Wrap the other end of the string around a pencil, making sure it is close to the cut edge of the background piece in the upper left corner, as shown in diagram 2. Carefully draw an arc from folded edge to folded edge. Make sure the string is snug, but not enough to move the straight pin. After the guide line is marked with a pencil, carefully trim away the excess fabric with scissors. Repeat step 3 for making the backing.

Diagram 1 ✱

4. Refer to the appliqué placement and the general instructions in the front of the book to fuse and position the appliqué pieces to the topper. Use a small zigzag stitch and matching thread around each shape to appliqué it to the table-topper top.

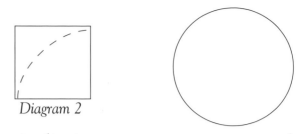

Diagram 2

5. Appliqué 7 acorns on seven tongues. With right sides together sew 21 tongue fronts to backs, leaving the bottoms open. Clip the curves and turn right side out. Carefully press and topstitch 1/4" from the edge of each tongue. You will have 7 acorn-appliquéd tongues and 14 plain tongues.

6. Place the 21 tongues evenly spaced around the edge of the table topper, as shown. Make sure when placing tongues that you have 2 blank tongues between the appliquéd tongues.

7. Pin the tongues right side down on the right side of table topper, as shown. Baste 1/8" from raw edge to hold in place.

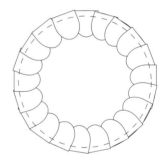

8. Place the backing and table topper with right sides together, and pin in place. Sew around the edge, using a 1/4" seam allowance. Leave an opening of approximately 8 inches for turning. Clip the curves, turn the table topper right side out, and press carefully. Hand-stitch the opening closed. Topstitch 1/4" from edge around the table topper.

WST. stitch 1/4" seam allowance leaving bottom open. Clip corners, turn and press. Top stitch 1/4" around tongue.

TABLE TOPPER
-*Tongue* (Trace 42)
-*Large Oak Leaf* (Trace 8)
-*Small Oak Leaf* (Trace 8)

53

ELK PENNY RUG
-Elk Head & Antlers (Trace 4 each)
-Large Acorn Top & Bottom (Trace 11 each)

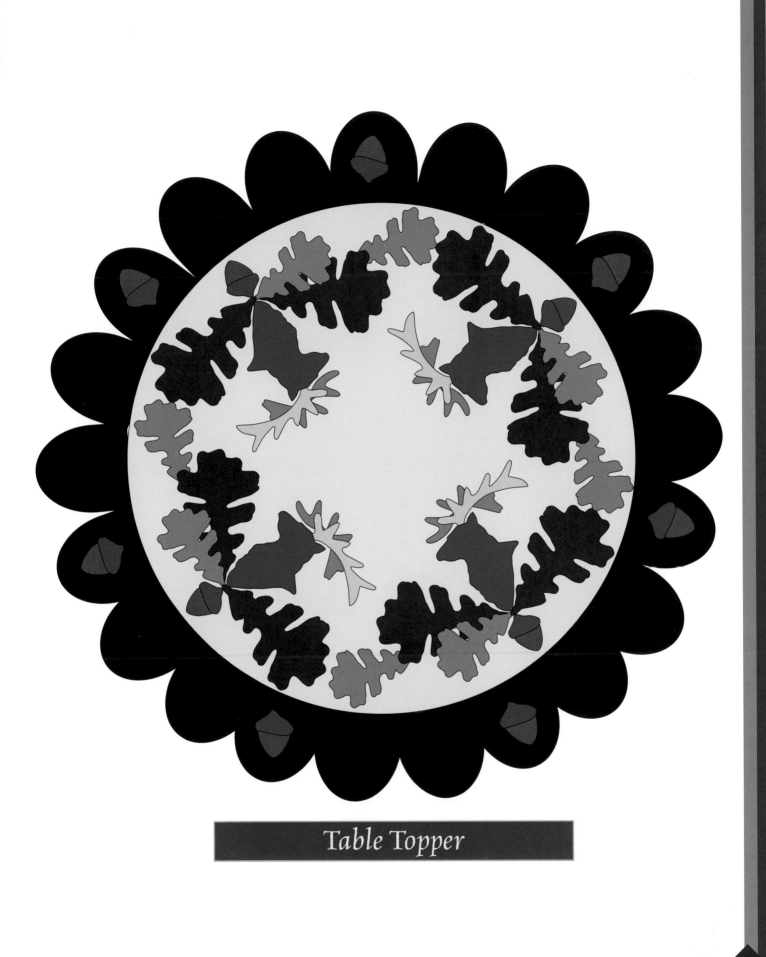

Table Topper

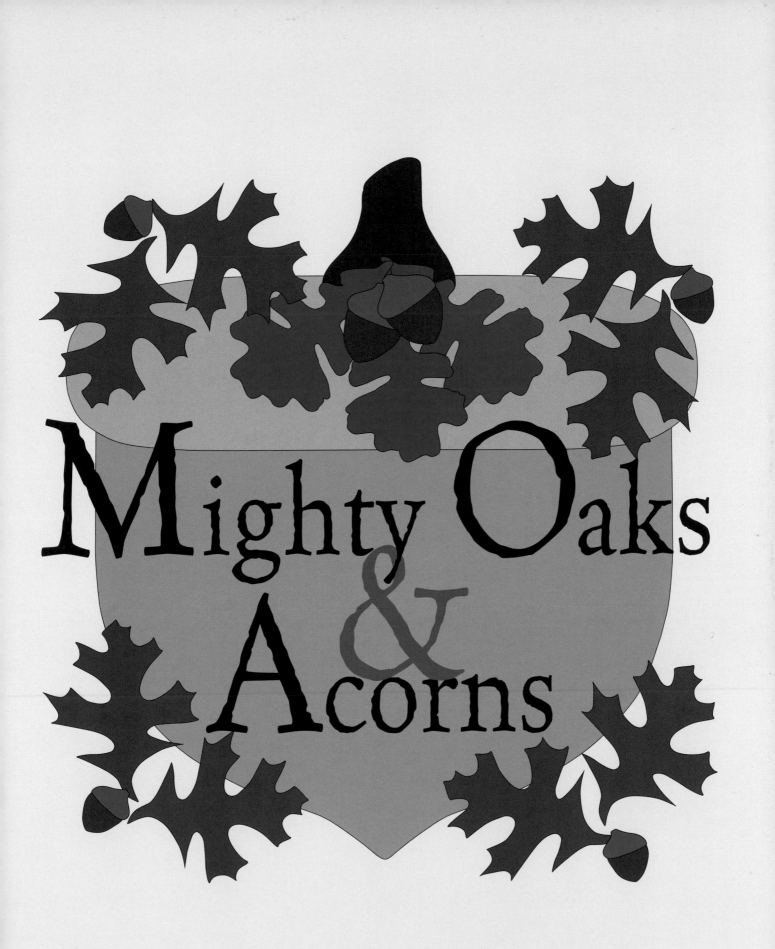

MATERIALS

NOTE: *Fabrics are based on 60" wide felted wool that has not been washed. Please purchase accordingly.*

2-3/4 yards	Background, Border and Binding Fabrics
3-1/2 yards	Backing
55" x 65"	Lowest Loft Batting
7 yards	HeatnBond®—Lite
Size 8	Perle Cotton (Assorted colors to match fabrics)

APPLIQUÉ FABRICS

Large Acorn Fabrics

1/2 yard	Tan Wool Felt for Large Acorn Bottoms
1/4 yard	Light Brown Wool Felt for Large Acorn Tops
6" x 9" piece	Dark Brown Wool Felt for Large Acorn Stem Bottoms
2" x 4" piece	Light Brown Wool Felt for Large Acorn Stem Tops

Small Acorn Fabrics

5" x 5" piece	Medium Brown or Light Green Wool Felt for Small Acorn Bottoms
5" x 5" piece	Dark Brown Wool Felt for Small Acorn Tops

Bear Block Fabrics

4" x 6" piece	Black Wool Felt for Bear
3" x 7" piece	Gray Wool Felt for Ground
1" x 1" piece	Gold Wool Felt Bear Nose
10" x 16" piece	Medium Green Wool Felt for Blueberry Leaves
5" x 5" piece	Blue Wool Felt for Blueberries
4" x 10" piece	Rust/Gold Wool Felt for Oak Leaves on Acorn

Buffalo Block Fabrics

4" x 4" piece	Brown Wool Felt for Buffalo Body
4" x 4" piece	Black Wool Felt for Buffalo Body Front and Head
3" x 9" piece	Lavender Wool Felt for Mountains
1" x 1" piece	Cream Wool Felt for Buffalo Horn
9" x 12" piece	Gold Wool Felt for Aspen Leaves
5" x 5" piece	Light Green Wool Felt for Aspen Stems
4" x 8" piece	Light Green Wool Felt for Oak Leaves on Acorn

Elk Block Fabrics

5" x 5" piece	Brown Wool Felt for Elk Body

3" x 4" piece	Dark Brown Wool Felt for Elk Head
3" x 3" piece	Cream Wool Felt for Elk Front Antlers
3" x 3" piece	Cream Wool Felt for Elk Back Antlers
2" x 2" piece	Cream Wool Felt for Elk Tail
2" x 7" piece	Brownish Green Wool Felt for Ground
4" x 8" piece	Light Green Wool Felt for Oak Leaves on Acorn
10" x 20" piece	Rust Wool Felt for Pin Oak Leaves

Fish Block Fabrics

5" x 5" piece	Green Wool Felt for Fish Body
2" x 2" piece	Light Green Wool Felt for Fish Mouth
3" x 3" piece	Brown Wool Felt for Fish Belly
1" x 1" piece	White Wool Felt for Fish Eye
6" x 7" piece	Dark Blue Wool Felt for Large Water
3" x 5" piece	Light Blue Wool Felt for Small Water
12" x 14" piece	Green Wool Felt for Pine Sprigs
4" x 10" piece	Orange Wool Felt for Pine Cones
4" x 8" piece	Rust Wool Felt for Oak Leaves on Acorn

Moose Block Fabrics

5" x 6" piece	Brown Wool Felt for Moose Body
3" x 4" piece	Medium Brown Wool Felt for Moose Head
3" x 4" piece	Cream Wool Felt for Back Rack
3" x 4" piece	Tan Wool Felt for Front Rack
4" x 10" piece	Medium Green Wool Felt for Oak Leaves on Acorn
8" x 16" piece	Dark Green Marble for Large Oak Leaves
2" x 6" piece	Blue Wool Felt for Ground

Wolves Block Fabrics

10" x 12" piece	Black Wool Felt for Wolves
3" x 7" piece	Green Wool Felt for Ground
8" x 16" piece	Dark Rust Wool Felt for Maple Leaves
3" x 3" piece	Gold Wool Felt for Moon

CUTTING INSTRUCTIONS

From Black Wool Felt:
- Cut 6—20" x 20" squares
- Cut 3 strips—5-1/2" x 60". Set aside for border.
- Cut 1 strip—9-1/2" x 60" for top border.
- Cut 4 strips—1-1/2" x 60". Set aside for binding.

Helpful Hints using Wool

1. Use an even-feed foot on your machine when sewing.

2. Lengthen the stitch when machine-sewing the blocks together and the borders on the quilt.

3. Press the seams open to reduce the bulk.

4. It may be necessary to use steam when fusing appliqué.

5. Use a utility stitch when hand-quilting the quilt. Utility or running stitches are stitches spaced farther apart.

ASSEMBLY

1. Refer to the appliqué placement and the general instructions in the front of the book to fuse and position the appliqué pieces to the quilt block. Use a hand blanket stitch and matching thread around each appliqué.

2. Sew the blocks together in 3 rows, as shown. Press seams open.

3. Sew the rows as shown. Press seams open to reduce bulk.

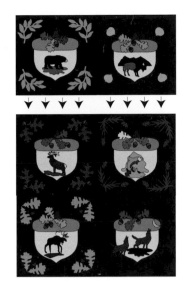

4. Measure the quilt top through the center lengthwise for the measurement of the side border strips. Cut 2 strips that length from the 5-1/2" x 60" border strips. Sew to each side and press seams open to reduce bulk.

5. Measure the quilt top through the center widthwise for measurement of the top and bottom border strips. Cut 1 strip that length from the 5-1/2" x 60" border strip and 1 strip from the 9-1/2" x 60" strip. Sew the 5-1/2" strip to the bottom and the 9-1/2" strip to the top. Press seams open to reduce bulk.

6. Refer to appliqué placement in the photo when fusing the appliqué pieces on the top border. Hand buttonhole stitch around each shape.

7. Layer the quilt backing, batting, and quilt top. Quilt using a utility stitch, and bind with 1-1/2"-wide strips of black wool felt.

Wool Quilt

Top Border
-*Pine Sprig* (Trace 8)
-*Pine Cones* (Trace 16)

(Reverse 4)

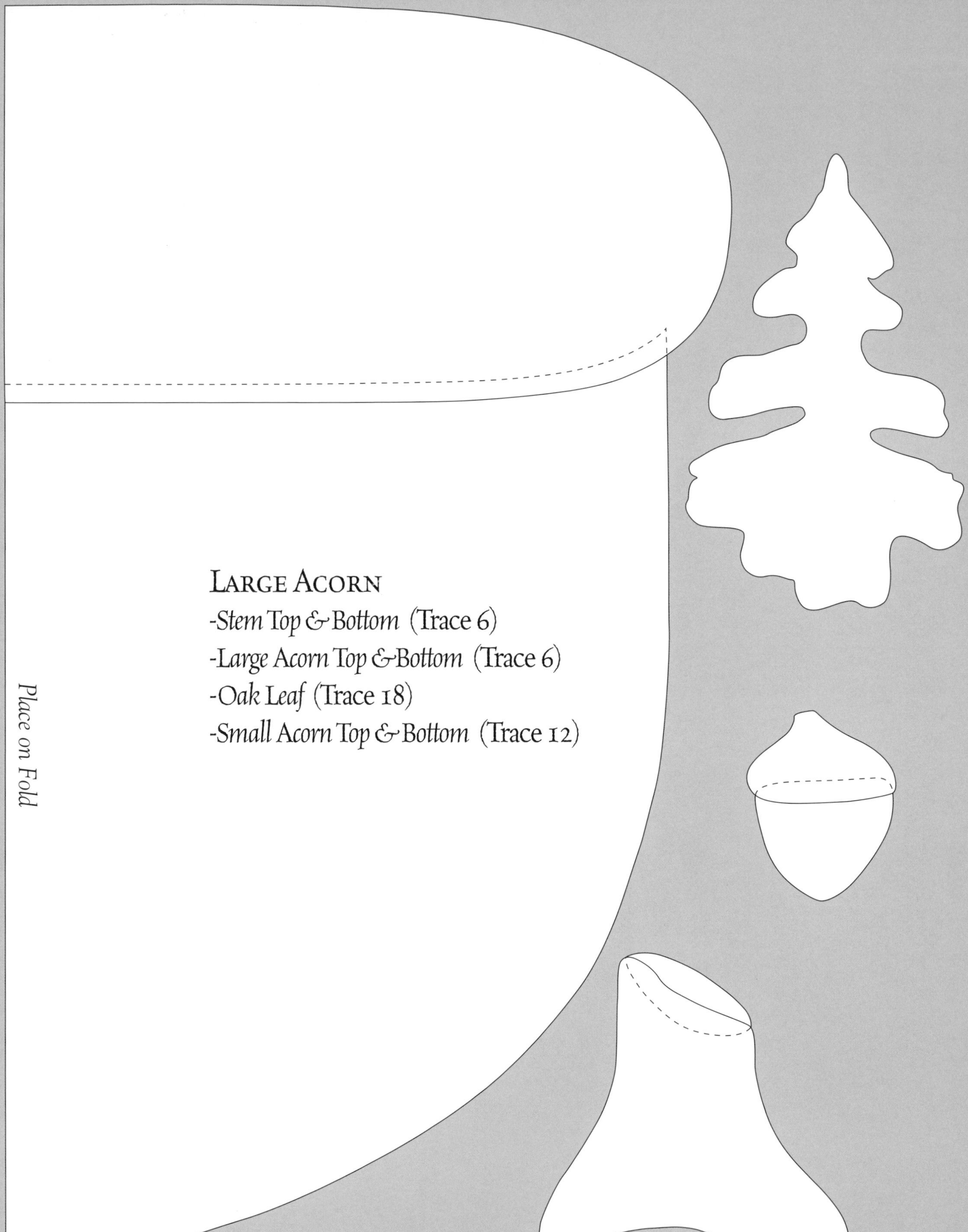

Place on Fold

LARGE ACORN

-*Stem Top & Bottom* (Trace 6)

-*Large Acorn Top & Bottom* (Trace 6)

-*Oak Leaf* (Trace 18)

-*Small Acorn Top & Bottom* (Trace 12)

(Reverse 3)

BEAR BLOCK
- Blueberries (Trace 24)
- Blueberry Leaves (Trace 6)
- Bear Body (Trace 1)
- Bear Nose (Trace 1)
- Ground (Trace 1)

Buffalo Block
-Aspen Stem (Trace 4)
-Aspen Leaves (Trace 12)
-Buffalo Body, Head & Horn (Trace 1)
-Mountain (Trace 1)

ELK BLOCK
-Acorn Top & Bottom (Trace 4)
-Elk Body, Head, Tail & Antlers (Trace 1)
-Pin Oak Leaf (Trace 8)
-Ground (Trace 1)

(Reverse 2)

FISH BLOCK
-*Pine Sprig* (Trace 4)
-*Pine Cones* (Trace 8)
-*Large Water* (Trace 1)

FISH BLOCK
-*Fish Body, Eye, Belly and Mouth* (Trace 1)
-*Small Water* (Trace 2)
-*Large Water* (Trace 1)

MOOSE BLOCK
-Moose Body, Head & Racks (Trace 1)
-Oak Leaf (Trace 8)
-Acorn Top & Bottom (Trace 4 each)
-Ground (Trace 1)

WOLF BLOCK
-Maple Leaf (Trace 8)
-Moon (Trace 1)
-Wolf (Trace 2)
-Ground (Trace 1)

Mighty Oaks & Acorns
Table Runner

(Finished size 15" x 37" approximately)

MATERIALS

3/8 yard	Tan Print for Background Fabric
1/2 yard	Dark Brown Marble for Border and Binding Fabric
2/3 yards	Backing
20" x 42" piece	Batting

APPLIQUÉ FABRICS

8" x 10" piece	Gold for Pin Oak Leaves
2" x 5" piece	Brown for Acorn Tops
2" x 5" piece	Medium Green for Acorn Bottoms
6" x 10" piece	Medium Green for Small Oak Leaves
10" x 12" piece	Dark Green for Large Oak Leaves
6" x 6" piece	Dark Brown for Center Square
6" x 12" piece	Dark Green for Outer Center Squares
1-1/4 yard	HeatnBond®—Lite

Sulky® threads to match appliqués

Stabilizer – Lightweight (Tear-away)

NOTE: *Fabrics are based on 42"-wide fabric that has not been washed. Please purchase accordingly.*

CUTTING INSTRUCTIONS

From Tan Print:
- Cut 1 rectangle – 12" x 34".

From Dark Brown Marble:
- Cut 3 strips – 2" x 42"; from strips cut 2 — 2" x 34" rectangles, and 2—2" x 15" rectangles.

ASSEMBLY

1. Sew a 2" x 34" Dark Brown Marble border strip on each side of the 12" x 34" background piece, as shown. Press toward the dark.

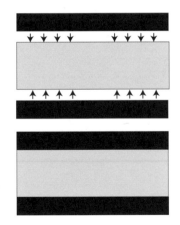

2. Sew the 2" x 15" Dark Brown Marble strips on each end of the quilt top, as shown. Press toward the dark.

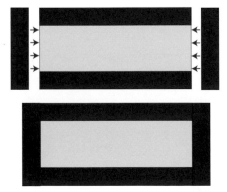

3. Refer to the appliqué placement and the general instructions in the front of the book to fuse and position the appliqué pieces to the quilt top. Use a small zigzag stitch and matching thread around each shape to appliqué it to the quilt top.

4. Layer the quilt backing fabric, batting, and quilt top. Baste the layers together. Hand-or machine quilt as desired. Finish the quilt by sewing on the binding, following the steps in the general instructions at the front of the book.

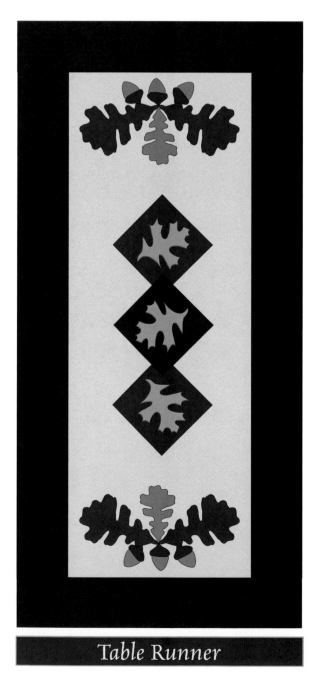

Table Runner

TABLE RUNNER
-*Small Oak Leaf (Trace 2)*
-*Large Oak Leaf (Trace 4)*

TABLE RUNNER
-Acorn Top & Bottom (Trace 6 each)
-Pin Oak Leaf (Trace 3)
-Square (Trace 3)

MATERIALS

Purchased Hand Towel

ELK APPLIQUÉ FABRICS

5" x 6" piece	Green for Oak Leaves
4" x 6" piece	Gold for Acorn Bottoms
3" x 3" piece	Brown for Acorn Tops
4" x 5" piece	Dark Brown Marble for Head
2-1/2" x 4" piece	Gold for Antler
2" x 4-1/2" piece	Dark Tan for Antler
1/4 yard	HeatnBond®—Lite

Sulky® threads to match appliqués

Stabilizer – Lightweight (Tear-away)

SPRIG APPLIQUÉ FABRICS

5" x 6" piece	Gold for Pine Cones
6" x 15" piece	Dark Green for Sprigs
1/4 yard	Heatn'Bond®—Lite

Sulky® threads to match appliqués

Stabilizer – Lightweight (Tear-away)

BUFFALO APPLIQUÉ FABRICS

10" x 10" piece	Brown for Body
10" x 10" piece	Black for Head
3" x 3" piece	Gold for Horn
1/3 yard	HeatnBond®—Lite

Sulky® threads to match appliqués

Stabilizer – Lightweight (Tear-away)

FISH APPLIQUÉ FABRICS

7" x 8" piece	Light Blue for Water
2" x 5" piece	Medium Blue for Water
2" x 5" piece	Dark Blue for Water
2" x 2" piece	Gold for Fish Head
7" x 7" piece	Medium Green for Fish Body & Fly
4" x 7" piece	Pumpkin for Fins & Fly
2" x 2" piece	Black for Hook
1/4 yard	HeatnBond®—Lite

Sulky® threads to match appliqués

Stabilizer – Lightweight (Tear-away)

NOTE: *Fabrics are based on 42"-wide fabric that has not been washed. Please purchase accordingly.*

ASSEMBLY INSTRUCTIONS

1. Refer to the appliqué placement and the general instructions in the front of the book to fuse and position the appliqué pieces to the towel.

2. Use a small zigzag stitch and matching thread around each appliqué piece.

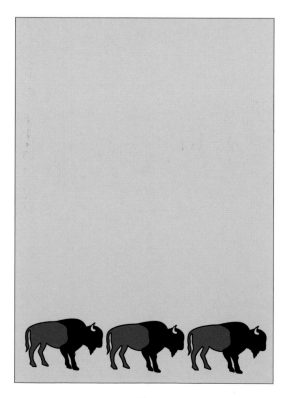

ELK TEA TOWEL

-Acorn Top & Bottom (Trace 3 each)

-Oak Leaf (Trace 2)

-Elk Head & Antlers (Trace 1 each)

PINE SPRIG TEA TOWEL
-*Pine Cone* (Trace 6)
-*Pine Sprig* (Trace 2)

(Reverse 1)

BUFFALO TEA TOWEL
-*Buffalo Body, Head & Horn* (Trace 3 each)

80

FISH TEA TOWEL

-*Fly & Hook* (Trace 1 each)
-*Fish Body, Head & Fin* (Trace 1 each)
-*Small Water* (Trace 2)
-*Large Water* (Trace 1)

Mighty Oaks & Acorns
Pinecone Runner

(Finished size 20" x 42" approximately)

MATERIALS

1/2 yard	Black Felted Wool for Background Fabric
1 yard	Flannel for Backing Fabric
25" x 47" piece	Low-Loft Batting
1 yard	Lightweight Fusible Web
Size 8	Perle Cotton in assorted colors to match fabrics

APPLIQUÉ FABRICS

24" x 24" piece	Sage Green Felted Wool for Pine Sprigs
10" x 10" piece	Rust Felted Wool for Pinecones

NOTE: *Fabrics are based on 60"-wide wool that has been felted. Please purchase accordingly.*

CUTTING INSTRUCTIONS

From Black Felted Wool:
- Cut 1 rectangle – 12-1/2" x 44-1/2".

ASSEMBLY

1. Refer to the appliqué placement and the general instructions in the front of the book to fuse and position the appliqué pieces to the runner. Use a hand buttonhole stitch and matching thread around each shape.

2. Layer batting, backing flannel (right side up) and wrong side up of table runner. Sew around the table runner using a longer stitch length, leaving an opening at one end. Trim off excess backing and batting. Clip corners and turn right side out. Press carefully. Whip stitch opening closed. Stitch 1/2" from the edge of the table runner, using a utility stitch.

Helpful Hints using Wool

1. Use an even-feed foot on your machine when sewing.

2. Lengthen the stitch when machine-sewing.

3. It may be necessary to use steam when fusing appliqué pieces to runner.

4. We used a utility stitch when hand-quilting 1/4" around finished harvest table runner. A utility stitch is a longer stitch, on the order of a folk-art or primitive stitch.

5. Felted wool is 100% wool that has been washed in hot water/cold rinse, then dried on hottest setting in a dryer. This washing/drying method shrinks and tightens the fibers allowing us to use the wool for rug-hooking, quilting, and appliquéing in quilt projects. Always ask if purchased wool is felted, or you can felt your own using above felting suggestions. Hand-dyed felted wools give a unique variation of colors to any quilt project.

WOOL HARVEST TABLE RUNNER
-*Pine Cones* (Trace 11)
-*Sprigs* (Trace 6)

Pinecone Runner

Tablecloth

(Tablecloth size 40" x 40")

MATERIALS

1-1/4 yards	Light Green Print for Background Fabric
1-1/4 yards	Backing

APPLIQUÉ FABRICS

18" x 22" piece	Dark Green Marble for Leaves
18" x 22" piece	Light Green Marble for Leaves
8" x 8" piece	Brown Marble for Acorn Top
10" x 10" piece	Gold Marble for Acorn Top
7/8 yard	HeatnBond®—Lite

Sulky® threads to match appliqués

Stabilizer – Lightweight (Tear-away)

NOTE: *Fabrics are based on 42"-wide fabric that has not been washed. Please purchase accordingly.*

CUTTING INSTRUCTIONS

From Background:
- Cut 1 square - 40" x 40".

From Backing:
- Cut 1 square - 40" x 40".

ASSEMBLY

1. Refer to the appliqué placement, and the general instructions in the front of the book to fuse and position the appliqué pieces to the tablecloth top. Use a small zigzag stitch and matching thread around each shape to appliqué it to the tablecloth top.

Helpful Hints for Appliqué Placement

1. Mark the center of the tablecloth with a straight pin. Place the large oak leaves approximately 3" from center straight pin. Each small oak leaf is placed at clock positions 12, 3, 6, and 9.

2. When large oak leaves are positioned, place small oak leaves and acorns next. Place 3 leaves and 3 acorns in each corner.

3. Lay the tablecloth top and backing with right sides together, and pin them in place. Sew around the edges, using a 1/4" seam allowance. Leave an opening of 8-10 inches for turning. Trim the corners, turn the tablecloth right side out, and press carefully. Hand-stitch the opening closed. Topstitch 1/4" from fold edge around all edges.

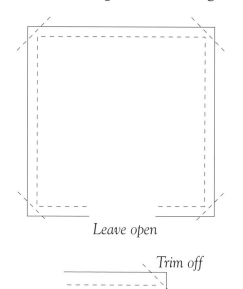

Leave open

Trim off

OAK LEAF TABLECLOTH
-*Large Oak Leaves* (Trace 16)
-*Small Oak Leaves* (Trace 12)
-*Acorn Tops & Bottoms* (Trace 20 each)

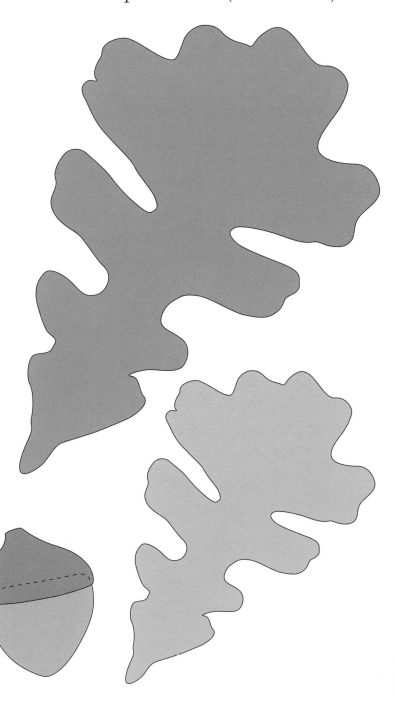

Oak Leaf Tablecloth

(Finished size 60" x 81" approximately)

MATERIALS

1-7/8 yards	Tan Print for Background Fabric
2-1/8 yards	Dark Brown Marble for Sashing, 1st Border, 3rd Border, and Binding
1/2 yard	Gold, Medium Brown, Dark Brown, Light Green, and Dark Green Marble for 2nd Border Fabrics (5 of each color)
5-1/4 yards	Backing
Full Size	Batting

APPLIQUÉ FABRICS

18" x 22" piece	Brown Marble for Elk Body
10" x 12" piece	Dark Brown Marble for Elk Head
9" x 9" piece	Tan Print for Elk Front Antlers
8" x 8" piece	Medium Brown Marble for Elk Back Antlers
1/2 yard	Medium Brown Marble for Pin Oak Leaves
1/4 yard	Dark Green Marble for Small Oak Leaves
1/4 yard	Light Gold Print for Large Acorn Tops

1/2 yard	Light Green Marble for Large Acorn Bottoms
6" x 9" piece	Medium Brown Marble for Acorn Stem Bottoms
2" x 4" piece	Dark Brown Marble for Large Acorn Stem Tops
5" x 5" piece	Dark Brown for Small Acorn Tops
5" x 5" piece	Medium Brown for Small Acorn Bottoms
1/8 yard	Dark Green Marble for Ground
6 yards	HeatnBond®—Lite

Sulky® threads to match appliqués

Stabilizer – Lightweight (Tear-away)

NOTE: *Fabrics are based on 42" wide fabric that has not been washed. Please purchase accordingly.*

CUTTING INSTRUCTIONS

From Tan Print:
- Cut 3 strips—20" x 42"; from strips cut 6—20" x 20" squares.

From Sashing, 1st Border, 3rd Border, and Binding Fabric:
- Cut 18 strips – 2-1/2" x 42".
- Cut 8 strips 3" x 42". Set aside for Binding.

2nd Border:
- Cut 8 strips 1-1/2" x 42" from each fabric.

ASSEMBLY

1. Refer to the appliqué placement and the general instructions in the front of the book to fuse and position the appliqué pieces to the quilt block. Use a small zigzag stitch and matching thread around each shape to appliqué it to the quilt block.

2. After the quilt blocks are appliquéd, resquare the blocks and trim so all 6 blocks are the same size.

3. Measure the quilt blocks through the center and cut 3 strips that length from 2 of the 2-1/2" x 42" sashing strips.

4. Sew the sashing strips to the appliqued blocks, as shown. Press toward the dark. You will have 3 rows of 2 blocks and a sashing strip.

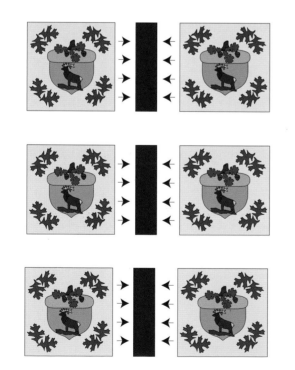

5. Measure the sashing rows through the center for sashing length. Use 4 strips from the Dark Brown Marble 2-1/2" x 42" sashing strips and cut to the length needed. Sew the rows together, as shown *above right*. Press toward the dark.

6. Measure the quilt top lengthwise through the center for the measurement of the side border strips. Diagonally piece 4 Dark Brown Marble 2-1/2" x 42" strips and cut the strips to the correct length. Sew the strips to the sides and press toward the dark, as shown *below*.

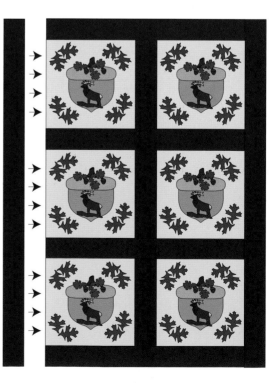

7. Arrange 5 of the 2nd border 1-1/2" strips in a pleasing manner. Sew the strips together in opposite directions, as shown, to avoid a curved strip. Press the strips in one direction carefully to avoid stretching. You will need 8 of Unit A.

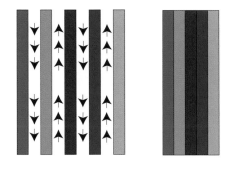

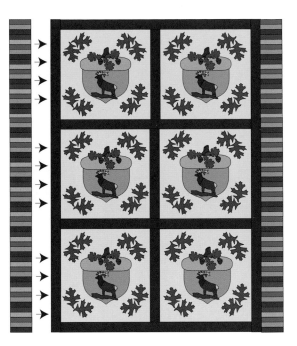

8. Cut Unit A into seven 5-1/2" x 5-1/2" squares, as shown. You will need 52 of Unit B.

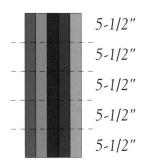

5-1/2"
5-1/2"
5-1/2"
5-1/2"
5-1/2"

Sew 14 of Unit B together for each side border and 12 of Unit B together for top and bottom border. Press carefully to avoid stretching the strip.

NOTE:
It may be necessary to remove and/or add rectangles to the borders to get the needed length to fit the quilt top. Remember to add or remove the rectangles on the same end of both strips so they are identical.

9. Measure the quilt top lengthwise through the center for the side border measurement. Cut the length needed from the pieced 2nd border strips. Sew to each side and press toward the dark carefully.

10. Measure the quilt top widthwise through the center for the measurement of the top and bottom border strips. Cut the length needed from the pieced 2nd border strips. Sew to the top and bottom and press towards the dark carefully.

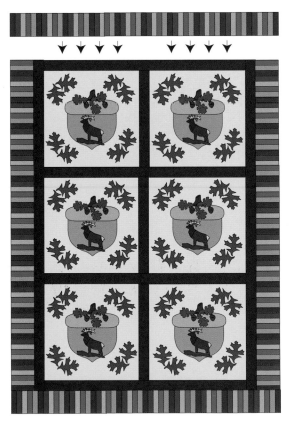

11. Measure the quilt top lengthwise through the center for the measurement of the side border strips. Diagonally piece 4—2-1/2" x 42" Dark Brown Marble Strips and cut the strips to the correct length. Sew the strips and press toward the dark.

12. Measure the quilt top widthwise through the center for the measurement of the top and bottom border strips. Diagonally piece 4—2-1/2" x 42" Dark Brown Marble strips and cut the strips to the correct length. Sew the strips to the top and bottom and press toward the dark.

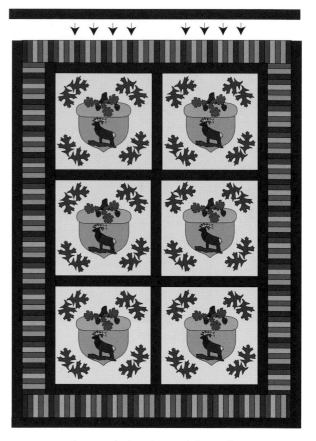

13. Layer the quilt backing fabric, batting, and quilt top. Baste the layers together. Hand or machine-quilt as desired. Finish the quilt by sewing on the binding, following the steps in the general instructions at the front of the book.

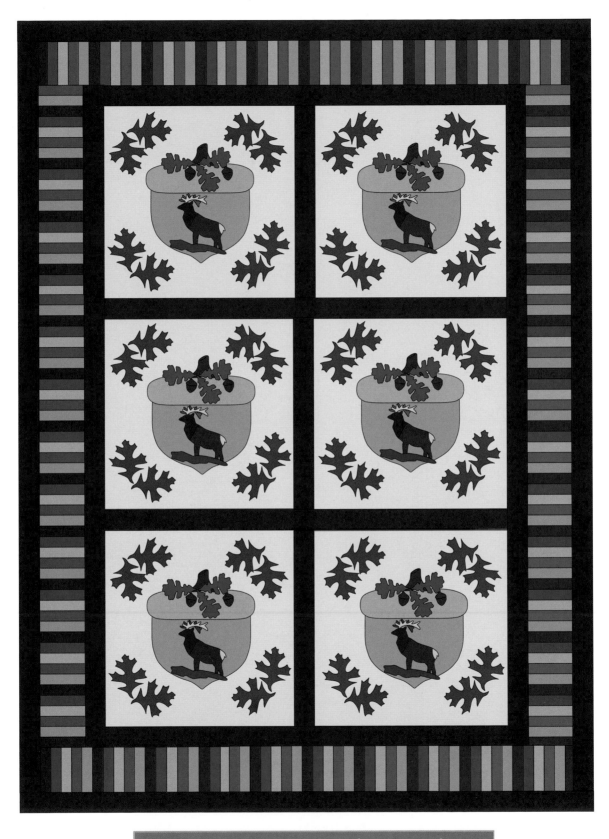

Piano Keys Border Quilt

LARGE ACORN
-*Stem Top & Bottom* (Trace 6)
-*Large Acorn Top & Bottom* (Trace 6)
-*Oak Leaf* (Trace 18)
-*Small Acorn Top & Bottom* (Trace 12)

ELK BLOCK

-Acorn Top & Bottom (Trace 12 each)
-Elk Body, Head, Tail & Antlers (Trace 6 each)
-Pin Oak Leaf (Trace 48)
-Ground (Trace 6)

Nature's Splendor
On-Point Snuggler

(Quilt size 50" x 62" approximately)

MATERIALS

1-1/4 yards	Tan Print for Squares
1-1/4 yards	Blue Marble for Squares
1/2 yard	Brown Marble for 1st Border
1-1/8 yards	Nondirectional Fabric for 2nd Border, *or*
2-3/8 yards	Tree Print for 2nd Border
3/4 yard	Tree Print for Binding
3-1/3 yards	Backing
58" x 70" piece	Batting

APPLIQUÉ FABRICS

1/4 yard	Gold Print for Pin Oak Leaves
5" x 5" piece	Light Tan for Horn
18" x 22" piece	Black for Buffalo Head
18" x 22" piece	Brown Marble for Buffalo Body
1 yard	HeatnBond®—Lite

Sulky® threads to match appliqués

Stabilizer – Lightweight (Tear-away)

NOTE: *Fabrics are based on 42"-wide fabric that has not been washed. Please purchase accordingly.*

CUTTING INSTRUCTIONS

From Tan Print:
- Cut 5 strips 6-7/8" x 42"; from the strips cut 24—6-7/8" x 6-7/8" squares. Diagonally cut squares to make 48 triangles.

From Blue Marble:
- Cut 5 strips – 6-7/8" x 42"; from the strips cut 24—6-7/8" x 6-7/8" squares. Diagonally cut squares to make 48 triangles.

From Brown Leaf Print:
- Cut 5 strips—2-1/2" x 42".

2nd Border Fabric (Nondirectional):
- Cut 6 strips—5-1/2" x 42".

2nd Border (Directional):
- To be cut later in directions.

Binding:
- Cut 7 strips—3" x 42".

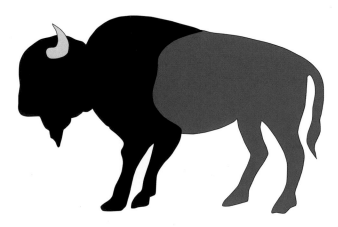

ASSEMBLY

1. Sew the Blue Marble and Tan Print triangles together, as shown. Press toward the dark. You will have a total of 48 half-square triangle units.

2. Sew 2 half-square triangle units together, as shown. Press in the direction of least amount of bulk.

Make 24

3. Sew 3 of Unit A together, as shown. Press in the direction of least amount of bulk.

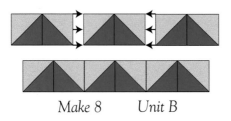

Make 8   *Unit B*

4. Sew 2 of Unit B together, as shown. Press in the direction of least amount of bulk.

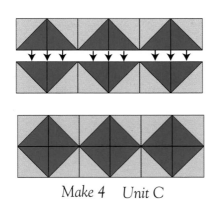

Make 4   *Unit C*

5. Sew each Unit C together to form 4 rows, as shown. Press in the direction of least amount of bulk.

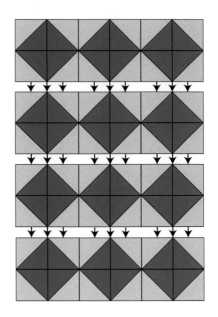

6. Measure the quilt top widthwise through the center for the measurement of the top and bottom border strips. Cut the length needed from the brown leaf print 2-1/2" x 42" strips. Sew the strips to the top and bottom. Press toward the dark.

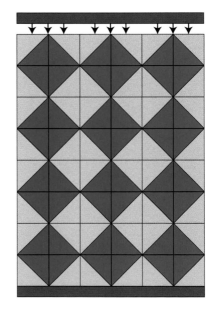

7. Measure the quilt top lengthwise through the center for the measurement of the side border strips. Diagonally piece and cut the length needed from the brown leaf print 2-1/2" x 42" strips. Sew onto each side of the quilt. Press toward the dark.

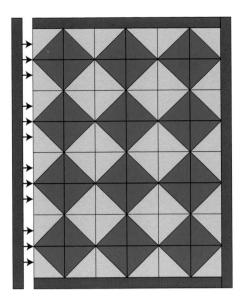

10. Measure the quilt top lengthwise through the center for the measurement of the side-border strips. From fabric cut 2 strips lengthwise of the tree fabric 5-1/2" x length of the side border strips.

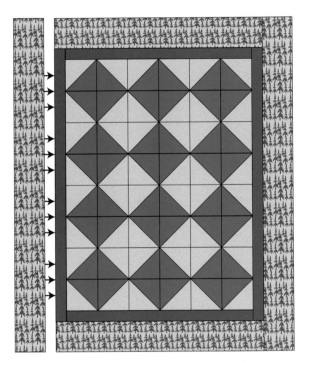

Sew the strips to each side, making sure to have design facing up. Press toward the dark.

8. Repeat Steps 6 and 7 if using nondirectional fabric for 2nd border.

9. Directions for 2nd border using directional fabric:
   • Cut 2 strips – 5-1/2" x 42".

Measure the quilt top widthwise through the center for the measurement of the top- and bottom-border strips. Cut the 5-1/2" strips to length needed and sew to the top and bottom of the quilt.

NOTE: *Remember to sew the strips with design facing up on top and bottom strips.*

Press toward the dark.

11. Refer to the appliqué placement, and the general instructions in the front of the book to fuse and position the appliqué pieces to the quilt top. Use a small zigzag stitch and matching thread around each shape to appliqué it to the quilt top. Remember to use tear-away stabilizer for stitching appliqués.

12. Layer the quilt backing fabric, batting, and quilt top. Baste the layers together. Hand- or machine-quilt as desired. Finish the quilt by sewing on the binding following the steps in the General Instructions in the front of the book.

ON-POINT SNUGGLER

-*Buffalo Head, Body & Horn*
   (Trace 6 each, Reverse for 3 Buffalo)
-*Pin Oak Leaf (Trace 14)*

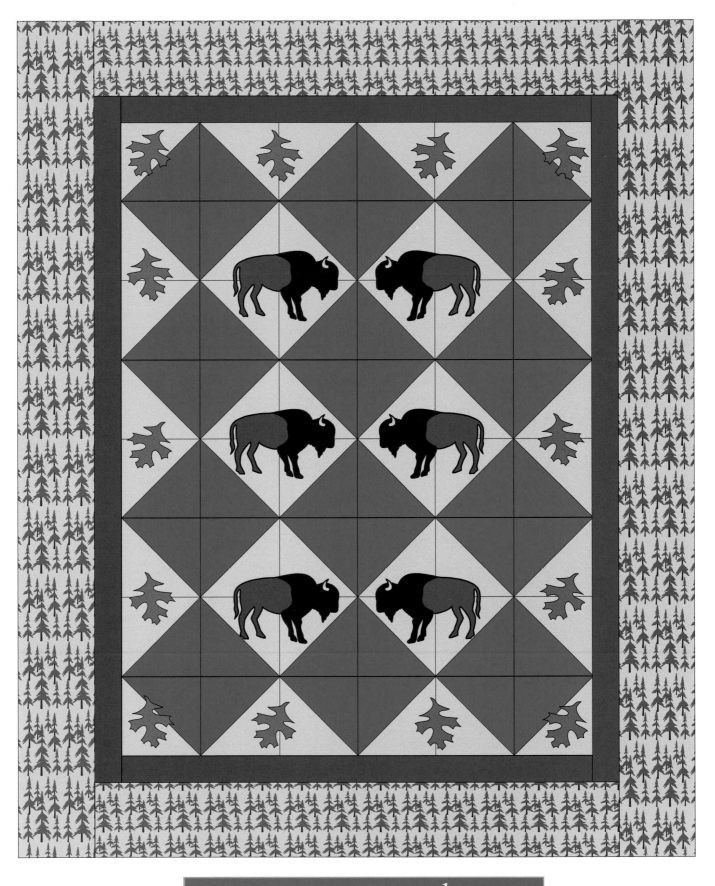

On-Point Snuggler

Nature's Splendor
Wallhanging

(Wallhanging size 20" x 42" approximately)

MATERIALS

3/8 yard	Tan Print for Background Fabric
1/2 yard	Plum Marble for Border
3/4 yard	Black Marble for Border
1-3/8 yards	Backing
25" x 47" piece	Batting

APPLIQUÉ FABRICS

1/8 yard	Black for Buffalo Head
1/8 yard	Brown Marble for Buffalo Body
4" x 4" piece	Light Tan for Horns
1/4 yard	Deep Plum for Large Mountains and one Small Mountain
1/8 yard	Lavender Marble for two Small Mountains
1/6 yard	Green Marble for Tree Line
1-1/4 yards	HeatnBond®—Lite

Sulky® threads to match appliqués

Stabilizer – Lightweight (Tear-away)

NOTE: *Fabrics are based on 42"-wide fabric that has not been washed. Please purchase accordingly.*

CUTTING INSTRUCTIONS

From Tan Print:
- Cut 1 rectangle—12" x 34".

From Plum Marble:
- Cut 6 strips—1-3/4" x 42".

From Black Marble:
- Cut 3 strips—1-3/4" x 42".
- Cut 1 strip—4-1/4" x 42"; from strip cut 4—4-1/4" x 4-1/4" squares.
- Cut 4 strips—2-1/2" x 42". Set aside for binding.

ASSEMBLY

1. Sew a Plum Marble 1-3/4" x 42" strip on each side of a Black Marble 1-3/4" x 42" strip, as shown. Press toward the dark.

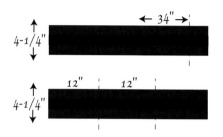

Make 3

2. Cut two 4-1/4" x 34" rectangles and two 4-1/4" x 12" rectangles, as shown.

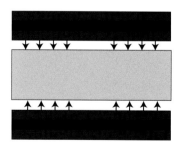

3. Sew a 4-1/4" x 34" Unit A on each side of the 12" x 34" Tan Print piece, as shown. Press toward the dark.

4. Sew a Black Marble 4-1/4" square to each end of the 4-1/4" x 12" rectangles from Step 2, as shown. Press toward the dark.

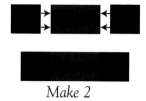

Make 2

5. Sew the Unit B sections from Step 3 to each end, as shown. Press toward the dark.

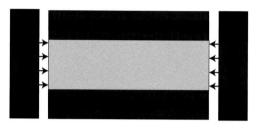

6. Refer to the appliqué placement and the General Instructions to fuse and position the appliqué pieces to the quilt top. Use a small zigzag stitch and matching thread around each shape to appliqué it to the quilt top.

7. Layer the quilt backing fabric, batting, and quilt top. Baste the layers together.

8. Hand- or machine-quilt as desired. Finish the quilt by sewing on the binding, following the steps in the General Instructions.

BUFFALO WALLHANGING

-*Buffalo Head, Body & Horn* (Trace 4 each)
-*Tree Line* (Trace 4)

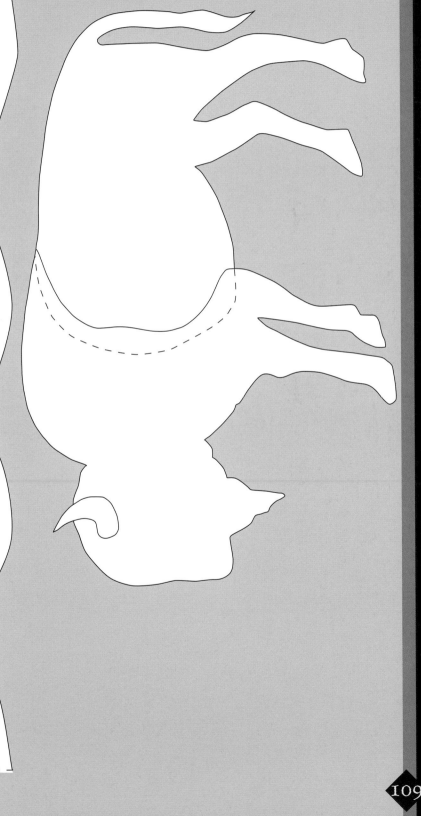

LARGE ACORN

-*Large Mountains (Trace 2)*
-*Small Mountain (Trace 3)*

Wallhanging

Corner Block Wallhanging

(Finished size 30" x 30" approximately)

MATERIALS

5/8 yard	Blue Print for Background Fabric
1/4 yard	Brown Marble for 1st Border Fabric
1/2 yard	Navy Marble for Triangle Square Units
2/3 yard	Blue Print for Triangle Square Units and Outer Squares
3/8 yard	Navy Marble for Binding
1 yard	Backing
35" x 35" piece	Batting

APPLIQUÉ FABRICS

18" x 22" piece	Brown Print for Big Horn Sheep
4" x 4" piece	Light Tan Print for Horns and Tail
3" x 7" piece	Brown Marble for Tree Trunks
18" x 22" piece	Navy Batik for Mountains
18" x 22" piece	Sage Green Marble for Trees
1 yard	HeatnBond®—Lite

Sulky® threads to match appliqués

Stabilizer – Lightweight (Tear-away)

NOTE: *Fabrics are based on 42"-wide fabric that has not been washed. Please purchase accordingly.*

CUTTING INSTRUCTIONS

From Blue Print:
- Cut 1 square 18-1/2" x 18-1/2".

From Brown Marble:
- Cut 2 strips 1-1/2" x 42"; from the strips cut 2—1-1/2" x 18-1/2" rectangles and 2—1-1/2" x 20-1/2" rectangles.

From Navy Marble:
- Cut 2 strips 5-7/8" x 42"; from the strips cut 8—5-7/8" x 5-7/8" squares. Diagonally cut squares to make 16 triangles.

From Blue Print:
- Cut 2 strips 5-7/8" x 42"; from the strips cut 8—5-7/8" x 5-7/8" squares. Diagonally cut once for 16 triangles.
- Cut 1 strip 5-1/2" x 42"; from the strips cut 4—5-1/2" x 5-1/2" squares.

From Binding:
- Cut 4 strips 2-1/2" x 42".

ASSEMBLY

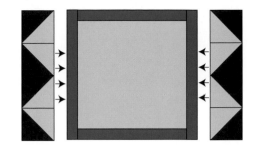

1. Sew the 1-1/2" x 18-1/2" Brown Marble 1st border strips to the top and bottom of the background piece, as shown. Press toward the dark.

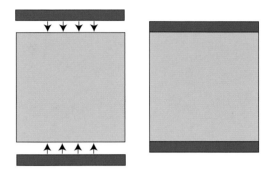

2. Sew the 1-1/2" x 20-1/2" Brown Marble 1st border strips to each side of the quilt top, as shown. Press toward the dark.

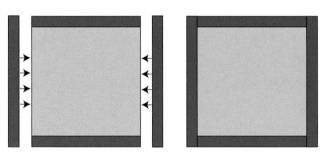

3. Sew the Navy Marble and Blue Print triangles together, as shown. Press toward the dark.

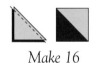

Make 16

4. Sew 4 half-square triangle units together, as shown. Press in the direction of least amount of bulk.

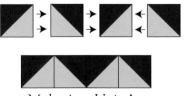

Make 4   Unit A

5. Sew 2 Unit A Strips to the sides of the quilt unit, as shown.

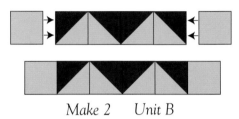

6. Sew the Blue Print 5-1/2" squares to each end of the remaining 2 Unit A units, as shown. Press toward the square to reduce bulk.

Make 2   Unit B

7. Sew Unit B to the top and bottom of the quilt, as shown. Press toward the dark or in the direction of least amount of bulk.

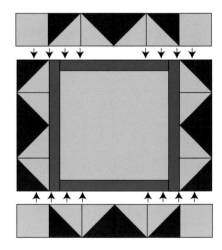

8. Refer to the appliqué placement and the general instructions in the front of the book to fuse and position the appliqué pieces to the quilt top. Use a small zigzag stitch and matching thread around each shape to appliqué it to the quilt top.

9. Layer the quilt backing fabric, batting, and quilt top. Baste the layers together. Hand-or machine-quilt as desired. Finish the quilt by sewing on the binding, following the steps in the general instructions at the front of the book.

CORNER BLOCK WALLHANGING

-Mountains (Trace 2)

CORNER BLOCK WALLHANGING

-Tree (Trace 4)

-Sheep Horns, Body & Tail (Trace 2 each)

-Large Tree Trunk (Trace 2)

-Small Tree Trunk (Trace 1)

Corner Block Wallhanging

Nature's Splendor
Legends Quilt

(Finished size 80" x 96" approximately)

MATERIALS

3-1/4 yards	Medium Brown Print for 6" squares and Set-in Triangles
2-1/8 yards	Tan Print for Pieced Blocks
2-1/8 yards	Dark Brown Floral for Pieced Blocks
3/4 yard	Dark Brown Print for 1st Border
1-3/8 yards	Dark Brown Floral for 2nd Border
1 yard	Dark Brown Print for Binding
6 yards	Backing
Queen Size	Batting

NOTE: *Fabrics are based on 42"-wide fabric that has not been washed. Please purchase accordingly.*

CUTTING INSTRUCTIONS

From Medium Brown Print:
- Cut 12 strips—6" x 42"; from the strips cut 80—6" squares.
- Cut 3 strips—9" x 42"; from the strips cut 9—9" squares. Diagonally cut each twice for 36 triangles.
- Cut 1 strip—4-3/4" x 42"; from the strips cut 2—4-3/4" x 4-3/4" squares. Diagonally cut each once for 4 triangles.

From Tan Print:
- Cut 18 strips—3-5/8" x 42"; from the strips cut 198—3-5/8" x 3-5/8" squares. Diagonally cut each once for 396 triangles.

From Dark Brown Print:
- Cut 8 strips—2-1/2" x 42".

From Dark Brown Floral:
- Cut 8 strips—2-1/2" x 42".

Binding:
- Cut 10 strips—3" x 42".

ASSEMBLY

1. Sew the medium and dark print triangles right sides together, as shown. Press toward the dark. You will need a total of 396 triangle-square units.

2. Sew two triangle-square units together, as shown. Press in the direction of least amount of bulk. You will have a total of 198 of Unit A.

3. Sew 2 of Unit A together, as shown. Watch so that the units are sewn in the correct position. Press in the direction of least amount of bulk. You will need 99 Unit B.

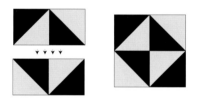

4. Sew the blocks together, diagonally, as shown in Diagram. Press in the direction of least amount of bulk. After the rows have been stitched together, sew the 4 corner triangles on. It may be necessary to trim off the excess triangles to square up the quilt top. When trimming the quilt top, make sure that you leave 1/4" seam allowance past the corners of the block, as shown.

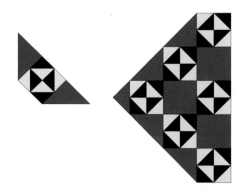

5. Measure the quilt top through the center widthwise for top and bottom border length. Diagonally piece and cut the Dark Brown Print 2-1/2" x 42" 1st border strips to that measurement. Sew to the top and bottom. Press toward the border. Measure the quilt top through the center lengthwise for side border length. Cut two strips that measurement and sew to the sides. Press toward the border.

6. Repeat Step 5 for second border.

7. Layer quilt top, batting, and backing. Baste and quilt as desired.

8. Diagonally piece the 3" binding strips together. Fold the strips in half, wrong sides together, and press. Stitch to the right side of quilt with raw edges matching. Fold over to the back and blind stitch, catching backing of quilt without piercing through to the front of the quilt.

Legends Quilt

Nature's Splendor
Legends Pillow

(Finished size 12" x 18" approximately)

MATERIALS

(Yardage listed is enough for 2 pillows.)

3/8 yard	Tan Print for Pieced Blocks and Center
1-1/2 yards	Medium Brown Print for Sashing and Back
1-1/8 yards	Dark Brown Floral for Pieced Blocks and Ruffle

APPLIQUÉ FABRICS

2" x 5" piece	Acorn Bottoms
2" x 5" piece	Acorn Tops
18" x 22" piece	Large Oak Leaves
6" x 10" piece	Small Oak Leaves
1-1/4 yards	HeatnBond®—Lite

Sulky® threads to match appliqués

Stabilizer – Lightweight (Tear-away)

NOTE: *Fabrics are based on 42"-wide fabric that has not been washed. Please purchase accordingly.*

CUTTING INSTRUCTIONS

From Tan Print:
- Cut 1 strip – 2-3/8" x 42"; from the strip cut 16—2-3/8" x 2-3/8" squares. Diagonally cut once for 32 triangles.
- Cut 1 strip – 6-1/2" x 42"; from the strip cut 2—6-1/2" x 12-1/2" rectangles.

From Medium Brown Print:
- Cut 2 strips—3-1/2" x 42"; from the strips cut 4—3-1/2" x 6-1/2" rectangles and 4—3-1/2" x 12-1/2" rectangles.
- Cut 2 strips—12-1/2" x 42"; from the strips cut 4—12-1/2" x 12-1/2" squares.

From Dark Brown Floral:
- Cut 1 strip—2-3/8" x 442"; from the strip cut 16—2-3/8" x 2-3/8" squares. Diagonally cut once for 32 triangles.
- Cut 5 strips—6-1/2" x 42"; from the strips cut 2—6-1/2" x 21" rectangles. Reserve 4 strips for ruffles.

ASSEMBLY

1. Sew the Tan Print and Dark Brown Floral triangles together, as shown. Press toward the dark.

Unit A
Make 32

2. Sew together 2 Unit A, as shown. Press in the direction of least amount of bulk.

Unit B
Make 16

3. Sew together 2 Unit B, as shown. Press in the direction of least amount of bulk.

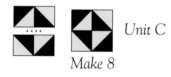
Unit C
Make 8

4. Sew the 3-1/2" x 12-1/2" Medium Brown Print sashing strips on the top and bottom of the center piece. Press toward the dark.

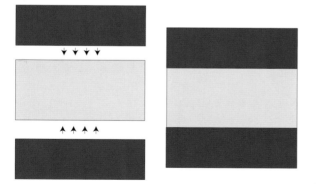

5. Sew the Unit C blocks on each end of the 3-1/2" x 6-1/2" Medium Brown Print sashing strips. Press toward the dark.

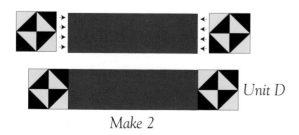
Unit D
Make 2

6. Sew one Unit D on each side of the pillow center. Press toward the dark.

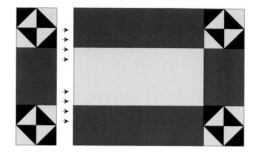

7. Refer to the appliqué placement and the General Instructions in the front of the book to fuse and position the appliqué pieces to the pillow top. Use a small zigzag stitch and matching thread around each shape to appliqué it to the pillow top.

8. Sew 2—6-1/2" x 43" Dark Brown Floral strips and 1—6-1/2" x 21" strip together to make a continuous ruffle strip. Fold the strip in half lengthwise, wrong sides together, and press.

9. Divide the ruffle strip into four equal sections and mark with safety pins. Sew two rows of basting stitches with the machine having the first basting row 1/8" from the raw edge and the second basting row 3/8" from the raw edge, as shown.

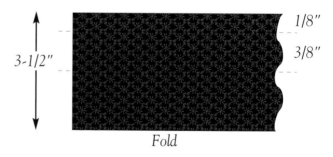
3-1/2"
1/8"
3/8"
Fold

10. Divide the pillow top into four equal sections and mark with safety pins. With right sides together, pin the ruffle to the pillow top, lining up the safety pins. Carefully pull the gathering threads until the ruffle fits the pillow top. Round the corners slightly. Sew the ruffle to the pillow top, stitching between the basting rows, as shown.

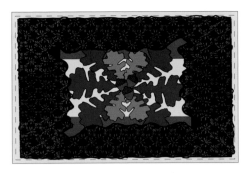

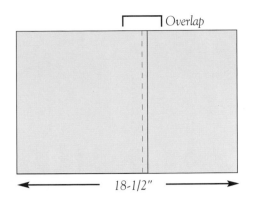

11. Sew 1/4" double hem on one edge of the 12-1/2" squares. Press.

12. Overlap two of the 12-1/2" Medium Brown Print squares so the pillow back measures 18-1/2", as shown. Pin together and baste 1/8" from raw edge to hold in place.

13. Pin the pillow top and back together, right sides together and sew. Be careful when sewing front and back together.

14. Turn the pillow right side out, insert a pillow form.

Legends Pillow

LEGENDS PILLOW
-Small Oak Leaf (Trace 4)
-Large Oak Leaf (Trace 6 each)
-Acorn Top & Bottom (Trace 3)

ACKNOWLEDGMENTS

I would like to extend a huge "thank you" to some special people for their support, talent, hard work, and dedication in making this book possible.

Thank you to:

Delores Farmer
Sue Carter
Sue Longville
Amy Gutzman
Kathy Geis
Suzy Peterson

Machine Quilting:

Cindy's Stitches (Cindy Kujawa)
All Things Quilted (Sharon Saunders)

Supply Sources:

Troy Corporation®
(Terry and Dorothy Troy)

An abundant supply of my fabric
lines for these quilt projects.

Husgavarna Viking
Sulky® Thread

Family Support:

A very special thanks to my husband, Mark. I appreciate the never-ending support and encouragement you've given me over the years. Another special thanks to my sons, Brad and Chad, and their wives, Jami and Jennifer, and granddaughter, Quinne. You all bring so much joy and happiness to my life.

Thank you to a few of my very special friends— my sisters, Dianne Pauls and Elizabeth Krautbauer—and my mother, Pat Segner, for all of your help, creative input, and outdoor fun.